The Seniority Solution

Your Road to a Reasonable Retirement

Gerry Stellwagen, CPA, CFP™

The Seniority Solution

Published by:
90-Minute Books
Newinformation! Inc
302 Martinique Drive
Winter Haven, FL 33884
www.90minutebooks.com
(863) 318-0464

Published in the United States of America

ISBN-13: 978-0692424889
ISBN-10: 0692424881

Here's What's Inside…

April 2015
Venice, FL

I wrote this book to help people who are retired or approaching retirement. There is so much information out there today about what to do in retirement – it's confusing. People often go to the wrong sources for key information. This is a simple book – no charts and graphs to confuse you – just a guide to show you all the things you should consider for a reasonable retirement. I tried to make it as conversational as possible – as if you and I were just talking it over.

To give you an example of how people can be misled, there's a person on TV who advertises that "none of my clients ever lost any money." That can sound great at first, but I know what he's selling, because I know what that phrase means. If you believe him and go to him for advice, you may end up making a big mistake. All he's doing is selling products that don't factor in taxes, inflation and extended-care needs. He's a salesman, not a financial planner.

There is another ubiquitous salesman who professes to hate the type of product that the aforementioned advisor is selling. He wants you to put all your money with him.

Neither one of them is right!

The whole point of this book is about planning and having somebody help you do a financial plan that makes sense for your needs and goals – something that's reasonable.

In a recent survey by the American Institute of CPAs, when asked to state the primary measure of financial success, the majority of respondents answered, "A Comfortable Retirement." I couldn't have said it better!

The stories and anecdotes throughout the book are designed to show you real life situations – both good and bad. The stories are true and I have witnessed them all. Of course the names are changed.

This book is designed to be a simple read – devoid of all the industry jargon. You won't see a discussion of "fat tails" or "kurtosis." I have deliberately eliminated charts and graphs and tables that can be confusing. My goal is not to impress you with fancy words, but to explain things in plain English.

I hope this book educates you and helps change your way of thinking about retirement planning.

Enjoy the book!

To your success!

Gerry Stellwagen

Chapter 1: How to Lose $700 Million

Thomas G. Plant was a turn-of-the-century entrepreneur. Starting his own company in the footwear business at the age of 27, he employed thousands of workers and developed a unique shoemaking process. His rise from shoe worker to shoe boss and eventually to company owner was unprecedented. The Thomas G. Plant Company flourished as a result of his vision and insight into the manufacturing process. The company made up to 3,000 pairs of shoes per day.

Tom eventually sold his business in 1910, and reportedly wound up with accumulated wealth estimated to be in excess of $20 million (close to $700 million in 2013 currency).

Plant started work on his estate, which would be "...a country home for a man of big thoughts and ideas, who can enjoy big things in a big way.' The estate, originally named Lucknow, and now known as Castle in the Clouds, covers 5,000 acres in the Ossipee Mountains on the shores of Lake Winnipesaukee. One thousand workers, many of whom were Italian artisans, constructed the home of tiles, marble, and exotic materials. They even incorporated an air-conditioning system, using the cool waters of a mountain stream.

In addition to his personal mansion, Plant decided to finance the construction of an exclusive country club, Bald Peak. Still in operation today, Bald Peak catered to the very wealthy and very socially acceptable people. The inability to attract members was the start of Plant's financial problems.

In 1917, Plant's investment in Russian bonds - some say upon the advice of frequent Lucknow visitor Teddy Roosevelt - became worthless. Similarly, a post-war boom in sugar led to a collapse, called La Danza de Los Milliones, when a formerly $100 share of Cuban cane sugar fell to 30 cents. Tom had invested heavily in the sugar markets. The depression of 1929 was the final nail in Plant's financial coffin.

Plant was allowed to live on his estate for his final years, assuming the role of caretaker. He died in 1941 at the age of 82; his few remaining friends took up a collection to bury his ashes.

What can we learn from the story of Thomas Plant?

To say he was headstrong is an understatement. He decided what he wanted to do and paid no attention to anyone else. His hubris, coupled with an extreme lack of diversification, was his downfall. Although it is not the author's purpose to examine the life of Thomas Plant, his life does provide a good example of how not to do it.

Plant's problems can be attributed to the following, which will be discussed in detail in later chapters:

- Living beyond one's means: Yes, even for someone worth three quarters of a billion dollars.

- Lack of diversification: Although we don't have all the figures, it is apparent that he went from a concentration in one bad investment (Russian bonds) to another (Cuban sugar).

- No rainy day fund or guaranteed investments: Certainly US government bonds were available. We have to assume that he craved the extra earnings of the Russian variety.

- Failure to take advice: Tom was a shoemaker, not a financier. A friend who was a financier, Philadelphian George Elkins, commented, "The goddamn fool, I told him not to buy them (the Russian bonds)."

This all transpired around the turn of the century. There was no such thing as a financial planner back then, but had I been there, I would have designed a detailed plan for him and had him diversify his investments. I doubt he would have listened, however. That's one of the problems today. I find that some men (and a rare woman or two) are just a little too macho. They won't listen. "Oh, I know. I was an executive with XYZ, and I know." That's a recipe for how to go wrong.

Tom was just headstrong. His friend, George, told him straight out not to buy the bonds. But Tom knew what was right, like a lot of people know they are right. I have a friend whose father made a lot of money. He's decided now to become a day trader. He's going to lose his money, too. It's the hubris that gets them.

Those people are not salvageable, unfortunately. I'm trying to talk to the more sane person who wants to do things right. I'm trying to give that person a roadmap to follow. I've seen too many mistakes made, and I want to help people steer clear of those mistakes.

A Contrast

Let me share with you another story to highlight this point. Not too far from Moultonborough and Lucknow lies the town of Laconia. It too, is on Lake Winnipesaukee, and it caters to many summer visitors, some with multi-million dollar mansions on the once unspoiled shores. Its year-'round residents are a hardy bunch, surviving the snow-laden winters with typical New England grit.

Just outside of town lives another millionaire; let's call him Bill. Like Tom Plant, Bill sold a business and cashed out. His fortune – while in the millions – was nowhere near the likes of Plant's; neither was his appetite for grandeur and high society.

At Bill's first meeting with a financial planner, the planner asked, "If you could invest your fortune in US Treasury bonds and maintain your lifestyle would you do so?" Bill's immediate response was: "Yes!" Then, after thinking about it for a moment, he admitted that he wanted to have a small investment in stocks, just because...So, on that day about 20 years ago, when Bill was 65, it was decided that his portfolio was to consist of 20% or so of low-cost, diversified mutual funds. The balance would be in fixed income instruments, most of which were guaranteed by the full faith and credit of the US Government. Over the years, he made investments in things like annuities and REITs to overcome the low interest rate environment. Bill has lived well below his means; his one concession was to update his home, a 19th century farmhouse, using local craftsmen and ordinary materials. He did, however, buy a new pickup truck – a Ford – which he traded in recently for...another Ford.

4

Fifteen years later, Bill's portfolio is approximately where it started. He has used the income and moderate growth – by design – to support his lifestyle. During the market crash of 2008 – 2009 his portfolio barely hiccupped. In fact, by rebalancing, he actually profited from the downturns; that's what happens when you have the time to recover. Bill will never run out of money. He also purchased a long-term care policy that will ensure his continued financial stability and protect his heirs.

When Bill sees an ad for an extravagant item – which he could well afford – his reaction is consistent; if he doesn't need it, he won't even consider it.

Bill's story is bland. No one wants to read about him, and that's just fine with Bill. He continues to live very comfortably, taking an occasional trip to Europe (economy class, of course) and spending a couple of weeks in Florida as a respite from the harsh New Hampshire winter. Bill is happy!

So ask yourself…who are you? Are you Bill or are you Tom? I hope that you're reading this book while you still have time to decide.

Bill is still humming along as this book goes to press. He's 85, and he's doing well. He doesn't have health issues. He doesn't have any anxiety or nervousness over what the stock market is or isn't doing. He isn't kept up late at night worrying that he will outlive his money. He's comfortable and happy, and I think that is where the real riches are.

Chapter 2: Planning Before Products

The old adage of putting the cart before the horse is very appropriate here. You need to plan before you invest. Clients often tell me at the first meeting that they have a certain lifestyle and want me to arrange their portfolio to accommodate that lifestyle. Sometimes it works and sometimes it doesn't. If they need to get a 10% return on their assets they will probably have to take too much risk. It's better to get some idea of what a reasonable portfolio can generate and plan your lifestyle accordingly.

Everyone has to file a tax return. It's required every year. You don't have to do a financial plan. You should, but nobody's saying, "If you don't have your financial plan done by April 15th, we're going to fine you." As a result, you put it off and put it off.

There's a strategy to doing the planning. You look at your resources and look at your goals and try to match them up. If you can prioritize your goals, you may be able to invest in enough low-risk assets to meet your necessities and take some more risk for other goals.

You really need to have a professional set up a plan for you – it's just too complex to do it on your own. Who will you choose to help you? A lot of so-called advisors are out there. Many with multiple designations and certifications, but it comes down to common sense.

You can find advisors online who have tens of thousands of clients and billions of dollars under their management. They spend fortunes advertising in national magazines and on TV. We now have what are called "robo advisors." You can go to their websites and have a portfolio designed for you with a few clicks of a mouse. You never talk to anybody during the process. One advisor wrote a book that you can use to score yourself on different factors and come up with a recommended portfolio.

That's just not going to work! You have to talk to somebody who knows what he or she is doing; you need a coach, a mentor or as we say, a "Partner." There are just no two ways about it. We'll discuss how to find the right person later on in the book.

Chapter 3: Income

You have to realize that income – cash income – is the only asset you can spend. You can't spend stocks. You can't spend bonds. You can't spend real estate. Everything, in order for you to get gain any use from it, has to be converted to income. One of the ways we help clients do that is by using a Bucket Plan™. There are three buckets – Now, Soon and Later.

In many cases, people have a portfolio with a brokerage house. They've had it for years while they're working. Then they retire and they just keep the same portfolio. Those portfolios are risky. When you are accumulating money, volatility doesn't hurt too much. But when you start to take income from your portfolio, volatility can be devastating.

In the Bucket Plan™, we schedule a period of time – the Soon bucket - to use part of your assets to buy some income. This can be accomplished in a number of ways: with annuities, short-term bond funds, bond ladders, Treasury bills or other instruments that have low risk and produce income.

Let's just say that for a 65-year-old, that period may be 10 years. This gives that 65-year-old 10 years to let his or her other assets grow and overcome inflation and hopefully be available to convert to income in the future.

Here's a description of the three buckets:

- The Now Bucket holds emergency funds – it's the amount that you want to be able to access at a moment's notice. It lets you sleep well.

- The Soon Bucket holds the assets that are going to produce income for you for a number of years, usually 8-12 years.

- The Later Bucket holds your long-term investments, like a mutual fund portfolio, a rental property – things that should keep up with inflation. It may also contain a long-term care insurance policy.

This plan mitigates the risk of retiring. With a traditional plan, if you retired just before the *The Black Swan*, you would be devastated. (That's a book that was written about the crash of 2008 and 2009.) You need to do some planning to make sure that doesn't happen to you. (Remember Bill? The market crash of 2008-2009 didn't have any effect on his retirement plans.)

Another thing we do in the planning stage is to subject your assets to a "stress test." We look at your portfolio and subject it to several scenarios, such as the market crashes noted above. Can you survive financially? It's a question that needs to be asked.

Chapter 4: Investment Risk

The markets go up and down.

The problem is that when you convert from investing to consuming, this volatility hurts you. If the bad returns come early in retirement, you have an issue. You can't just keep the same portfolio you've had while you were investing and accumulating. Now you're "decumulating" and it's a different world entirely.

Be careful of averages – don't rely on getting the average expected return every year. Some major investment companies will help you set up a retirement plan under the assumption that you will get the portfolio's expected return each and every year.

Simple numbers will tell you. I'm going to use extremes, because extremes make it easy to understand things. If you have a 50% return one year and a 50% loss another year – 50% up, 50% down – you would expect to be even. After all, your average return is zero. Consider this: If you have a $100,000 portfolio and have a 50% loss; you wind up with $50,000. Then you have your 50% gain - you only have $75,000. You don't have your original investment back. It works the other way too, if you get the gain first you still wind up with $75,000. Averages are very misleading. There's a saying: "You can drown in a pool that has an average depth of one foot." But if it's 20 feet down at the other end, it's easy to drown there.

I took on a client just before the "tech" crash of 2001 - 2002; she had been working with a popular local stockbroker. Her portfolio was almost entirely in equities and therefore quite risky. When she needed money for living expenses, the broker would take out a margin loan against those equities. That means she was leveraged. She didn't just have 100% in equity; it was more like a 120%, because she would still owe on that loan if the equities failed. Her broker didn't care. Giving her the loan meant that he didn't have to sell any of her assets; he could keep them under management and make money on them, in addition to making interest on the loan.

I got her out just before the crash. I was only doing what was right; I didn't know the crash was coming. We used part of her money to buy a lifetime annuity (her Soon bucket) which made her so happy. She got a check every month. With that check, her modest schoolteacher's pension and social security, she could easily meet her necessities. We put the rest of her money into a very conservative, market-based portfolio. She never worried about money again.

I encouraged her to upgrade her condo. She never felt she could spend anything; it took a while to convince her that she had the means to glass in her lanai so she could enjoy it during the hot Florida summers. I had been in contact with her children through the years, and when she passed, they came down to talk to me about the estate, There was money left over for them, yet she didn't go without. It was the Bucket Plan that gave her that comfort.

Mike and Art

I had two friends, both CPAs. We'll call them Mike and Art. Mike met a broker who told him, "I've got this system, and I can make a lot of money trading." I don't recall exactly what the system was; it may have been interest rate futures or some other exotic thing like that. Anyway, it worked – for a while.

Mike was a very conservative guy. He put a little bit of money in. To make a long story short, it worked so well for him that he made quite a bit of money. He put his retirement plan into the strategy, and it continued to perform well. Then he got a second mortgage on his house. Everything he had was in this program, and one day it crashed. He lost everything. He wound up losing his job and went on disability. He died a few years later of a massive heart attack.

He didn't have to do that. He was a smart guy. He had a good job with a big accounting firm; he had a good future ahead of him, but he couldn't resist the urge to make more money, for what reason, I don't know.

The other fellow, Art, was just the opposite; he wouldn't buy a share of IBM if you pinned him down and put a gun to his head. He wouldn't buy anything other than CDs and money market funds. He said, "I don't think I need to take any risk. I can have a nice living. I can have this kind of car. I'll keep it for five or ten years." When I talked to him about a year ago, he's still happy. He has his family, his grandkids, his own CPA firm, and he's financially content.

That's Tom and Bill all over again. The Toms and Mikes of the world act impulsively over these crazy schemes. Somebody gets in their ear. For Mike it was a shame. Everybody told him that it wouldn't work. It really wasn't the broker's fault. He thought he had a great system. He was investing in it, too, and he lost everything as well. Things just don't work like that. There is a relationship between risk and reward – no free lunch!

Active versus Passive Investing

In the general spectrum of things, there are two ways to invest in the stock market. With active management, money managers work to find the best stocks, the best mutual funds. They spend large amounts of money doing it. With passive management, the money manager will say, "Let's just buy the whole market and take what it gives us."

The active investor must constantly be changing the portfolio as one stock goes out of favor and another is chosen. This process creates additional expenses, not only in the form of management fees that are passed on to the shareholders, but also in "frictional" costs such as trading commissions and taxes.

It's not impossible to pick the best stocks. In fact, a lot of these managers will do well over a period of time, and then they will fade away. It's just hard to rely on them. I've tried those tactics. I typically experiment using a small amount of my own money. I keep coming back to passive management. If you believe that markets work, you understand that the price of a given stock is what it's worth today. It may go up or down depending upon future events; if you know the future you can certainly do well in the financial markets.

Passive doesn't mean just buying an index fund and sitting on the couch collecting dividends. The leading passive manager in the marketplace is Dimensional Fund Advisors (DFA). It spends its research money trying to figure out how markets work. In fact, one of its founders and board members, Eugene Fama, won the Nobel Prize in economics last year for his research. DFA finds the dimensions of risk for which investors get rewarded. Trying to find the best stock is a zero-sum game that DFA doesn't play.

DFA funds are inexpensive and are not available through stockbrokers – only through approved professional investment advisors.

DFA funds, as good as they are, are not immune to market crashes. That's why it's important to have the right mix of equities and fixed income instruments for your situation.

But before you consider a portfolio, you need to decide about that Soon bucket. What percentage should you have in guaranteed items? Annuities are popular today.

What percentage do you have in guaranteed items? That's an individual decision, and a critical one.

Whether you choose to take the active or passive route, there are other elements to consider. For example, the bulk of your account's volatility and performance will be determined by your allocations to the three major asset classes: stocks, bonds, and cash.

The next step is to allocate within each class. For example, in the stock category, there are large cap, mid-cap, small cap, growth, and value stocks. And there are different markets: domestic, foreign developed, emerging markets and frontier markets. In fixed income instruments, there are annuities, long-term, intermediate-term, and short-term bonds, as well as income-producing real estate.

By investing in a mix of these asset classes and markets you can decrease volatility considerably.

When we subject your portfolio to the stress tests, you will see how your portfolio mix will weather the storm.

Chapter 5: The Role of Annuities

Annuities are getting a tremendous amount of press. There are two kinds of annuities, variable and fixed. I'm not a great fan of variable annuities, which are basically mutual funds in an annuity "wrapper." Most of them are very expensive. They do provide certain benefits, but they're getting few and far between. Some of the big insurance companies are now trying to buy back annuities they sold years ago. They promised too much and the companies are concerned about the effects on their own income. If you get an offer to buy back your annuity, you probably don't want to sell it.

The big disadvantage of a variable annuity is that you're required to pay ordinary income tax rates when you withdraw the money. However, if you had invested in a mutual fund, you would pay capital gains rates. Capital gains rates can range from 0%-20%. Ordinary income tax rates may run twice that. If you buy regular mutual funds, and pass them on to your heirs, they get what's called a step-up in basis. They never have to pay the tax on any gains that accumulated while you held the assets. Not so with an annuity. If you're going to invest in the stocks-and-bonds market, avoid annuities; invest in a regular portfolio. While there are some variable annuities with income riders, the riders are meant as a safety net in case you lose value. If you want income, invest in something else.

Turning to the topic of fixed annuities, the word annuity simply means "pay annually." Social Security is an annuity; so is your employee pension. I have a pension from my former accounting firm. They went to an insurance company and bought me a plain vanilla life annuity. This type of annuity is safe. I get my check on the 10th of every month; I've been getting it for years. It's not going to go away until I do.

A fixed annuity is just that. It's fixed; it can't lose money (unless you surrender it too early). In a fixed index annuity the interest you receive is based on the performance of a stock market index. You don't own the stock market index; rather, the interest received from the insurance company is based on it. A lot of the people who only sell stocks and bonds are against these annuities and many of them write articles showing how an investment in an index fund is better. They miss the point – it's like comparing apples to oranges. You have to compare annuities to bonds or CDs. Most of the fixed annuities have income riders that guarantee an increase over a period of time. When you trigger the rider, you can get a guaranteed lifetime income either for you alone or jointly with another person. You can't outlive the annuity payments and you will still have the value that the annuity has grown to – the best of both worlds, it seems. (The value will likely decrease over time as your payments continue, but even if the value goes to zero, you will continue to get your annuity payments.)

Detractors say, "These are sold by salesmen. They make a commission, and that's why they sell them." They want you to invest with them, so they can earn a fee. Over the long run there isn't much difference between how advisors get paid.

The Elements of Risk

There are a number of risk factors to take into account.

In order to get your desired return, you have to take on a certain amount of risk. And everyone has his or her own risk tolerance. Risk tolerance can actually be measured, and if your tolerance factor won't "allow" you to take on a certain amount of risk, then you have another issue. At that point, you've got to do something. You need to cut down on your expenses, lower your lifestyle, or adjust your portfolio. You don't want to take on more risk than you can tolerate, because if the market goes down, you're going to be scared, and you're going to get out. Then you won't get back in until it goes back up. This is called selling low and then buying high and you will lose money in the process.

You have to examine your capacity to handle risk. If you have a portfolio designed to buy a big sailboat and it crashes (the portfolio, not the sailboat), then you buy a smaller sailboat. If the portfolio is designed to provide you with food and shelter and it crashes, that's a whole different story. That's your capacity for risk.

Chapter 6: Taxes

"Taxman" ~George Harrison

Let me tell you how it will be
There's one for you, nineteen for me
'Cause I'm the taxman
Yeah, I'm the taxman

Should five percent appear too small?
Be thankful I don't take it all
'Cause I'm the taxman
Yeah, I'm the taxman

I've been in the tax business since 1972. Tax rates used to be much higher. Just before I got into the business, the top marginal rate approached 90%, but you could write off everything. There were tax shelters that basically involved borrowing money that you didn't have to pay back. There were all sorts of schemes. You can't directly compare rates, but the rates now are relatively low. Just as a quick reference, the estate tax "exclusion" for a married couple is $10+ million, before you pay a dollar of estate tax. It used to be $60,000 many, many years ago. The top rate now is 40%, it used to be 55%.

People don't pay much attention to taxes. When I prepare their tax returns, they're not that concerned. They don't understand how much of a drain taxes are on their income. If somebody has an investment sitting on the side, producing dividends and capital gain distributions they don't really need, they can be paying a whole lot of unnecessary taxes. If they put that same money into an annuity, the taxes are all deferred. They can take money out and pay taxes, but they do it when they want to, as opposed to just paying every year.

An alternative is a tax-managed account. DFA has tax-managed funds that distribute much lower dividends and capital gains without sacrificing performance.

Social Security Taxation

When Social Security was established, we were promised that it would not be taxable. Eventually, 50% of it was made taxable - now, it's up to 85%. The percentage depends on your other income, so in the example I just gave, if a person has a large amount of dividends, there would not only be a tax on the dividends themselves, but also a higher tax on Social Security. This is because it's based on a formula that takes into account other income, such dividends, capital gains or interest. Deferring that income helps postpone having to pay some taxes. You may eventually have to pay them, but deferring them makes good sense, because you can earn on the taxes that were deferred.

Numerous people have large sums of money in IRAs, or "Individual Retirement Arrangements." (That's the term that appears in the tax code.) As IRA guru Ed Slott says, "This is tax-infested money." The reason for this is that you will always have to pay taxes on a part of it – up to 100% taxable. The tax is not only on what you invested, but also on your earnings. If you have $200,000 in an IRA, you don't have $200,000 you can spend. As we have said, income and cash are what you can spend. You don't have that much, because you have to pay taxes on it. If you die and leave it to your heirs, they have to pay taxes on it. You can't get away from it. Convert to a Roth? In all the analyses I've done it appears that a Roth conversion is a good idea if you want to benefit your heirs; otherwise it's like prepaying your taxes. (Of course your situation may be an exception – a financial planner can advise you.)

Many retirees make the decision to start businesses of their own. They sometimes buy into franchises after working for other people – who covered half of their employment taxes – all of their working lives. When you're self-employed, you pay 100% of those taxes yourself. That's 15% percent, and it's only partly deductible. It comes down to about 12% net on average. If you're in a 25% tax bracket and you're self-employed, you're really in a 37% bracket. This is a great example of how devastating taxes can be.

You used to be able to deduct all your medical expenses. Now, if you're younger than 65, you have to have medical expenses in excess of 10% percent of your adjusted gross income before any of them are deductible. If you're older than 65, the figure is 7.5%, but that's going to end after 2016, so everybody's going to need to have in excess of 10% of AGI for medical expenses to be deductible.

Minimizing Your Taxes

Large medical expenses are certainly not uncommon among seniors, and they can present opportunities for deductions. For example if a number of these medical expenses – such as hip replacement or non-emergency heart surgery – can be planned and scheduled during a single year, they can add up to overcome the 10% threshold.

While it may not work for everyone, grouping medical expenses can be a very effective way to manage tax obligations. It's not a complete solution, but it could help a bit. Of course you have to itemize deductions (the so-called "long form") in order to deduct medical expenses at all. With the standard deduction for an over-65 married couple at nearly $15,000, you will need to have a lot of medical expenses, taxes and mortgage interest to benefit from itemizing.

One of the most egregious taxes is the one on Social Security income. When the system was created in 1935, FDR promised that SS income would not be taxed. If Social Security were a commercial annuity, we would have developed what's known as an "investment in contract" for the premiums we paid. When we finally received payments from the system, a portion would be nontaxable. However, Congress gets around the tax laws by calling our contributions a tax.

And the social security tax on our income keeps getting higher. As of 2014, it was based on the first $117,000 of earnings. Gone are the days for most of us when we could expect an increase in our paycheck somewhere around April or May, when we had satisfied the FICA requirement.

A self-employed person who is subject to this tax pays a whopping 15.3% - almost $18,000 if the threshold is reached. Half of it is deductible, so the net effect is somewhere around 12% depending on his or her tax bracket.

Chapter 7: Social Security

Planning for social security income is a relatively new game. Over the last five years or so, many strategies have developed.

Depending upon your date of birth, your full retirement age (FRA) will vary around 66. If you start taking your withdrawals early, you will only get about 75% of the benefit that you would get at your FRA. However, if you wait until age 70, you will get 132% of that same figure. That's a big difference. Assume that your FRA benefit is $2,000/month. At 62, you get $1,500/month but at 70 you're entitled to $2,640/month. Of course you will get more months of withdrawals if you start early. If you are single it's pretty easy to figure a "break-even" point for various starting dates.

However, for a married couple, the answer is not so simple. There are multiple strategies (some say as many as 80) to receive maximum benefits. Even if both spouses wait until age 70 without using one of the available strategies, they will be leaving a lot of money on the table.

I recently did an analysis for a married couple – the difference over their expected lifetimes between taking benefits at the earliest date versus using a strategy called, "file and suspend" came out to over $400,000.

The strategies are complicated; it is necessary to have computer software programs to do a complete analysis. And social security planning has to be done as part of your overall financial plan. Your life expectancy and need for cash income also play an important part.

Chapter 8: Extended Care

Not having extended care insurance can be financially devastating. This is one of the areas that many so-called advisors ignore. I belong to a long-term care organization that provides me with extensive information and help. The one question they suggest asking yourself is: "If you're lucky, you're going to get old; do you think you might become frail as you age?" Of course, that possibility exists. What are you going to do?

I'll tell you the story of a couple who are my clients – wonderful, friendly people. He is the throes of Alzheimer's. Every time they come in to the office, he's worse than the last time. While he fades in and out he appears to be relatively happy most of the time. The wife, however, is not faring so well. They're proof that the disease may hurt the person who gets it to an extent, but it's worse for the caregiver. Unfortunately, they didn't purchase insurance to cover this eventuality nor did they invest in other asserts that might help. I don't know what's going to happen to them. Medicare doesn't pay anything to speak of for long-term care. Ignore this at your own peril.

Insurance is very expensive, but there are other products available. I'm acquainted with an individual who has $100,000 in a CD. I told him, "Look, you can take it from the CD, where you might earn 0.1%, and put it into a hybrid product." Without going into detail about how it works, if my client is in need of long-term care expenses, it would provide around $200,000. He can get back that $100,000 anytime he wants to. All it would take is a phone call.

What's happening is that the earnings on that money are paying for the insurance. It's all done internally. To my way of thinking, there's is no reason to not do this. However, if you're older, your multiple won't be as great, but you'll have something. You'll have at least 50% more than you had to begin with, so it's still worth it.

If you don't have adequate funds, you can plan for Medicaid. Many people don't like facing that prospect, thinking that it's a form of welfare. If you want to set aside money for your family, that might be an option to consider. You need to go to an elder-law attorney, and have him work with you to reach the best solution. Even if you don't take any action, it would be an informed decision to just take your chances. You can do that, but do it from a position of knowledge, not just haphazardly.

If you opt for either insurance or one of the hybrid products, if you ever do need long-term care someone from the company will be assigned to manage your care for you. Your wife or husband or other relative won't have the devastating experience of having your family arguing with one another over your care.

My favorite hybrid products are designed similarly to a life insurance product. Technically, it is life insurance, but it's designed to pay out in the event that long-term care is necessary. It's life insurance with a long-term care rider. If you die with it, your heirs inherit the money, and they get a little more than you put in. If you don't use it, it's still there. You won't earn anything on it, but in a sense you're earning a great deal, because it will pay you for long-term care. An annuity version is available as well.

If you have money sitting in a CD or money market account it seems like a "no-brainer" to put it into one of these hybrid products where you can get your premium back at any time.

Chapter 9: Veterans' Benefits

As a veteran, and chairman of the VA Committee at the local Elks Lodge, I've been working with my fellow veterans for quite some time. Several years ago, I learned about a benefit called "Aid and Attendance," which is basically a tax-free pension. This applies to veterans who spent at least 90 days on active duty, with one day of the 90 being during wartime. He or she is not required to have fought in a war or even to have been in a war zone. The entire tour could have been in Washington, DC. There must be a medical need, and the veteran must undergo certain tests for assets and income.

Although it will change, you can currently adjust your assets in a number of different ways to qualify for Aid and Attendance benefits. If you failed to qualify today because you had $100,000 too much in assets, you could transfer them to your son or daughter, and tomorrow you'd qualify. (While that would work for the VA benefit, it's not a good idea for a number of reasons, primarily the Medicaid 5-year look back rules.) Right now, a single vet with one dependent can get about $20,000 a year, tax-free. Two vets who are married to one another may be entitled to $35,000. (Might they get $40,000 if they divorce? I don't know.) As you can see, this is a valuable benefit, and virtually no one is aware of it.

I know a Marine sergeant who was living on a tiny pension, plus some Social Security, in a rented trailer. He didn't quite live in squalor, but was fairly close to it. He had some medical issues and was becoming dependent upon neighbors to shop and care for him. For such a proud man, this was very difficult. I helped him get the Aid and Attendance benefit. Thanks to this benefit, he was able to move into a beautiful assisted living community, where he has his own apartment, and meals and housekeeping are provided. His medical expenses are covered. He's now on top of the world. Between the Aid and Attendance payment, Social Security, and a small pension, he's able to pay for it. That extra benefit saved his life. That's a good outcome and even though I didn't make a dime, it's one of my proudest accomplishments.

Chapter 10: When Things Go Wrong

I have been an expert witness in a number of court cases involving investments. Typically, if the violation is egregious, the case is settled before it goes to trial. I remember one case in particular. Upon examining the papers, I told the attorney, "This is pretty clear. They forged the client's signature. This signature doesn't look anything like hers." A case like that doesn't go to trial. It's obvious; the insurance company sees it and, knowing they can't win, they settle.

Let's say that a client has invested with a stockbroker, and his account crashes with the economy during the economic crash of 2008. He feels that this was the broker's fault. It could have been. It depends on the facts and circumstances. He may have told the broker, "I want you to invest this very conservatively. I don't want to take a chance." In that case, it is the broker's fault. On the other hand, he may have said, "Here, make me a lot of money." In that case it's not the broker's fault. But how do you prove it's one or the other?

The way to avoid all of this is to have everything put into writing. Most brokers will not provide you any information on their letterhead. They know that it can come back to haunt them. Conversations take place on the phone or in an office. Insist on documentation and written confirmation of everything you request. Write down everything you discuss, and file it away. Keep your notes and documentation in a bound record book and keep it together with all relevant papers.

If you do this, and if you truly were wronged, you'll win in court. Also, if you go to an attorney and you show him all of the paperwork, and he tells you that the broker followed your requests and did what you told him to do, then you're spared the hassle and cost of going through a big trial and not getting anything out of it.

Chapter 11: Here's How to Find the Right Planner for You

Where have all the planners gone?
Long time passing.
Where have all the planners gone?
Long time ago!
Where have all the planners gone?
Money managers, everyone!

To make sure you have found the right planner, look for these basic elements, which I call the Three Es: Education, Experience, and Ethics. As with a three-legged stool, you need all three. Which one is most important? It doesn't matter. You need them all.

Education: Any planner should have a college degree. The primary planning designations are the CFP, ChFC and PFS. Each is a little different, but having at least one of them is a necessity.

Experience: In his book *Outliers: The Story of Success,* Malcolm Gladwell wrote that ten thousand hours of experience are needed to become an expert. That equates to five years of doing nothing but gaining experience or, more likely 10 years of working, assuming that half of the time is spent marketing and other pursuits.

Ethics: An individual may earn all of the degrees, put in all of the experience, and if that person is a crook, none of that matters. Many planners use the designations as a marketing ploy; they never really do any planning. They just say that they're planners. It's hard for people to discern that, but it's smart to say, "Show me a financial plan that you did for a client."

I'm aware of planners who have taken the CFP test three times before earning the designation. Now that they do have it they use it to market themselves as certified financial planners, but they never have put together a plan. A person can be ethical, can be on the client's side, but if they don't have the education or the experience, they're going to be just as bad as the guy who's a crook.

I put together this chart to showcase the new way versus the old way of financial planning:

OLD WAY	NEW WAY
EMPLOYER	**CLIENT**
Broker-dealer, bank or insurance company hires salesperson to sell products (many of which are produced by the employer) to customers	Hires advisor to research, prepare, implement, and monitor integrated financial and investment plans based on a clear understanding of the client's goals, objectives, and values
SALESPERSON	**INDEPENDENT ADVISOR**
An employee or registered representative owing allegiance to employer.	Works for client in a fiduciary capacity owing a duty of utmost good faith.
CUSTOMER	**VENDOR**
Buys products and services as the result of salesperson's activities.	Producers of products and services selected by CLIENT and ADVISOR to provide optimal implementation of client's financial and investment plan.

Here's a story to highlight the differences between the old way and the new way. In 1972, I was working in the Financial Planning Division of the Tax Department of Peat, Marwick, Mitchell, and Company in New York. As CPAs, we prepared financial projections and did tax planning. In those days, estate taxes were a big issue, with a top rate of 55% and an exemption equivalent of $60,000. Today's exemption equivalent is more than $5 million per person.

Our wealthy clients needed planning to protect their estates. While we did the planning, one of the "blue shoe" law firms did the legal work, a "captive" insurance agent provided whole life insurance, and a '"customer's man," or stockbroker, from a Wall Street firm provided investments.

With certain clients, we would meet with the attorneys and the insurance agent to ensure that all of our suggestions were meshed and were compatible.

Fast forward to today. While there are still some captive agents and, of course, numerous stockbrokers, the once clear lines have blurred. With the exception of the lawyers, the other three disciplines are intertwined.

It's the age of the "financial advisor." This is a term that has no real significance, although most of the large stockbrokerage firms have adopted it. Some of these advisors do nothing more than recommend portfolios of mutual funds or stocks and bonds and then occasionally rebalance them. The only planning done is a cursory risk tolerance questionnaire and maybe a few projections. That's a far cry from the comprehensive financial planning provided by a true financial planner.

Fee-Only

Advisors who sell only stocks and bonds (including mutual funds) will try to tell you that they are conflict-free. They're not ... they can't provide all of the available products that people might need. In my opinion, they lack the ability to put the whole plan together

"Fee-Only" is a marketing term that some advisors have latched onto as the *sine qua non* of advisor purity. They have duped many financial writers, and even consumer organizations, about the preference of this method of providing financial advice.

Their pitch goes something like this: "We do not receive commissions from third parties; the only earnings we get are fees that we bill to you." Is the advisor's method of compensation the most important issue? I think not; ask the clients of Bernie Madoff, the most notorious fee-only advisor of recent note.

Some of this fee-only crowd will make arrangements with an insurance agent to provide life insurance for the client; the trade-off is that they expect referrals back from the insurance agent. So, the client is receiving investment advice for a fee and paying a commission for insurance products; he is not doing it with just one advisor, but with two. The danger here is that the fee-only advisor may not understand all the nuances of insurance products. Not being in the business, he or she does not know what is available. It's left up to the insurance agent to select the products and, while the advisor may have a fiduciary obligation to the client, the insurance agent most likely doesn't. The advisor has lost control!

A far better compensation method is the so-called "fee-based" arrangement, which I have incorporated into my practice. I provide financial planning and investment products for a fee and insurance products (life insurance and annuities) for a commission. I have access to virtually all financial products and can put together a complete portfolio for my clients. As an investment advisor, I have that fiduciary obligation, and it extends to all products that I recommend. The client is much better served.

Don't be fooled by an advisor's claim to work on a fee-only basis. Ask questions based on the information provided above. Better yet, find a planner with a fiduciary responsibility who can provide both planning and a full range of products to complement the plan.

Above all, don't pay attention to the talking heads on TV or to newspaper articles. They know nothing about you and have no obligation to you; if you follow their advice, you'll have no recourse.

Remember the words of Paul Simon:

"I don't believe what I read in the papers – they're just out to capture my dime."

Dime? I guess I've dated myself!

NAPFA

The National Association of Professional Financial Advisors is a small group (2,400 out of 71,000 Certified Financial Planners) that requires its members work on a "fee-only" basis. For some reason, the CFP Board has embraced this group and its policies, but it's just another marketing ploy.

I was a member of NAPFA for a while and was not impressed by their "holier than thou" attitude. In fact, I think that some of them are fee-only because they can't pass the securities exams.

Two of NAPFA's former Chairmen have been sanctioned by the SEC and the courts. *One of them was just sentenced to 16 years in federal prison, having been convicted of 32 criminal counts.* Of course numerous other advisors of all different stripes have had legal problems so the whole organization can't be scorned. The point is, don't rely on designations, organizations or methods of compensation when choosing an advisor; belonging to a particular organization or having certain initials after his or her name doesn't guarantee that this person is an honest advisor. Do your homework, starting with Broker Check (Google it), to at least see if an advisor has a checkered past. Other sources are the Better Business Bureau and the National Ethics Association.

Chapter 12: Epilogue

Walt Kelly (1913-1973) and his famous poster for the first Earth Day on April 22, 1970

You don't want to repeat the line from the Pogo cartoon shown above. Don't be your own worst enemy. You've got to look at your lifestyle. You can't just say, "I want to live this way now. Put my investments in something that makes 12% a year." That's a recipe for disaster.

You've got to look at all these areas. You might be going along really well, and then a long-term care issue comes up that you didn't plan for. You're going to be out of luck. You've got to be diligent. Look for the right advice and examine things. Don't take someone else's word for it. Don't listen to ads or talking heads on television, because if you do and lose your shirt, you have no recourse. They're not giving advice; it's just information.

It would be great if you could do it on your own, but you can't, not today. It might have worked to be your own planner 20 years ago, but there's just too much information to sift through these days. I have 40 years of experience, and I still learn something every day. I spend probably 20% of my time learning, and that's just to keep up. Find a planner you can trust, look at what they've accomplished, kick their tires, so to speak, and don't think that you're invincible, because you're not.

If you would like to work with me, I have an office in Venice, Florida. Our website is www.StellwagenandAssociates.com. Our phone number is 941-375-2171. I will give anybody a half hour without charge to discuss their situation.

I like to start out with people early in the year, so we can do their taxes (currently, our Senior Preferred Rate is $79 – most of our clients pay this amount) and I can get a feel for what their tax situation is. The first meeting is typically a conversation. During that conversation I try to figure out exactly what they want to do, what kind of resources they have, and how they feel about things. I like to learn about their children, their grandchildren, what their lifestyle is, and what they want to accomplish.

During the second meeting, we work out a preliminary plan. I run some options by them. I'm talking about design planning at this point, rather than product. If I see an issue, I may tell the person, "What you want to spend and what you have don't match. You need to do something else." If the person is still working, I may advise him or her to work longer and/or to save more. Those who have retired are told that they should cut back wherever possible to avoid running out of money. That doesn't happen very often. More often, what happens is that they've made several investments and have no idea what they have; they have no idea of the risk. If the market crashes again they don't have protection. Long-term care is another important consideration. It's important to bring up everything that may not be in place.

Once we get all of that taken care of, we can begin to put together a retirement plan. The plan covers all of the issues described in the preceding paragraphs; contains a timeline; and includes tax and cash flow schedules. Basically, the plan lays out the rest of the client's life; as well as we can predict it. Then we implement it, adding the right products and having regular meetings. Usually, during the first year, we'll have as many meetings as the client desires, but it's typically two or three meetings. After that, we meet at least once a year, usually around tax time, when they bring their tax information in.

We do charge a fee for developing the plan, and that includes future tax returns. It's not very costly, depending on the extent of the necessary work. Then we provide the products, as well as the reporting. We become their family's Chief Financial Officer.

Here's How to Get Your Roadmap to a Reasonable Retirement

You already know that people are living longer than ever before. The frightening part of this is not knowing whether or not you will outlive your money.

You need to protect yourself from growing old and frail without having a plan for extended-care costs.

That's where we come in. We will help you create a roadmap that will act as a financial guide throughout your lifetime.

Step 1: At no charge to you, we'll spend 30 minutes discussing your current situation. Then we can decide if it will be advantageous for us to work together.

Step 2: We'll walk you through our unique planning process to show you how we would design your roadmap.

Step 3: We'll design your roadmap, taking into account your financial needs, wants, and wishes. We'll stress test your investments and make recommendations that are designed to help you accomplish your goals with minimal risk.

Most people think it takes gambling in the stock market to retire well. Nothing could be further from the truth. While a conservative stock market portfolio may play a part, other assets can contribute greater stability and confidence.

If you'd like us to help you, just send an email to: gfs@wealthadvisors-llc.com or call us at 941-375-2171.

Visit our website at www.StellwagenAndAssociates.com.

About the Author

GERARD F. STELLWAGEN
CPA/PFS, CFP, CLU, ChFC, CLTC

Gerard F. (Gerry) Stellwagen has more than 40 years' experience in financial services. He started his business career at the international accounting firm of Peat, Marwick, Mitchell, and Company in New York City. During his 11 years as a practicing CPA, he attained the status of Tax Partner, with primary responsibilities for numerous individual and business clients, including politicians, top executives of Fortune 100 companies, and many owners of closely-held businesses. He's been published often in professional journals, and has co-authored a book on taxation that is used by the AICPA as part of a training course for CPAs.

In the early 1980s, Gerry entered the then-fledgling financial planning arena. He was intrigued by the ability to not only advise clients about taxes, but to also be conversant in other financial matters, such as insurance and investments.

During the last 24 years, Gerry has worked in a variety of roles. However, all of them have dealt with what is now known as "Wealth Management." Simply put, Wealth Management is the art and science of helping people of means get control of their assets and achieve their goals for themselves and their families.

Gerry holds the following designations/licenses:

Certified Public Accountant (CPA) in Florida and New York
Personal Financial Specialist (PFS)
Certified Financial Planner™ (CFP)
Chartered Life Underwriter (CLU)
Chartered Financial Consultant (ChFC)
Certified in Long Term Care (CLTC)

He is an Investment Advisor Representative of Prosperity Capital Advisors, a US Securities and Exchange Commission (SEC) Registered Investment Advisor, headquartered in Westlake, Ohio. Stellwagen & Associates is an A+ member in good standing of the Better Business Bureau. Gerry is a member of the National Ethics Association and the American and Florida CPA societies.

The Bucket Plan™ is trademarked intellectual property of C2P Mastermind Group.

Stellwagen & Associates
Tax and Wealth Advisors